GARFIELD
ON THE TOWN

BY: JIM DAVIS
and Lorenzo Music

BALLANTINE BOOKS • NEW YORK

ISBN: 0-345-31542-1

Designed and created by Jim Davis
Illustrated by Mike Fentz and Kevin Campbell
Cover designed by Mike Fentz
Manufactured in the United States of America

First Edition: October 1983
   2   3   4   5   6   7   8   9   10

GARFIELD
ON THE TOWN

GOOD MORNING,
MORNING

AND THEY SAY PETS ARE THERAPEUTIC

BOYS, BOYS, BOYS. JUST LOOK AT THIS ROOM

WHAT AM I GOING TO DO WITH YOU TWO? CRUELTY TO ANIMALS COMES TO MIND...

A ONE WAY TICKET TO THE CITY POUND SEEMS LIKE A GOOD IDEA

THE VET!

NOW SIT STILL, GARFIELD

THAT'S A GOOD BOY

JON? WHAT HAPPENED?

DR. WILSON

HI, DOC, THIS IS JON ARBUCKLE, YOU KNOW, GARFIELD'S OWNER

GARFIELD, WHAT NOW?

WELL, HE'S BEEN GONE FOR A WHILE, AND I WAS AFRAID HE MIGHT HAVE BEEN HIT BY A CAR

IN THAT CASE, YOU WANT A TOW TRUCK

WELL, THANKS FOR YOUR CONCERN

BOY, IT'S STARTING TO GET DARK. NO SWEAT, I CAN TAKE CARE OF MYSELF. IN FACT IT MIGHT BE KIND OF FUN TO GET INTO A LITTLE RUMBLE JUST TO LOOSEN UP

JUST LET SOMEONE TRY SOMETHING. I'LL GIVE 'EM THE OL'...HI-YA!

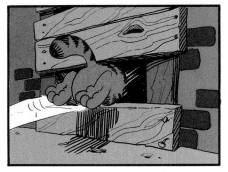

NOW I REMEMBER EVERYTHING

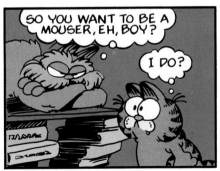

LET THE GAME BEGIN!

WE HAVEN'T HAD TROUBLE WITH THEM FOR A LONG TIME. I WONDER WHAT THEY WANT?

I THINK I CAN GUESS

WHAT DO YOU WANT?

LARDBALL!

THEY WANT SOMEONE CALLED, "LARDBALL"

LARDBALL?

WHO'S LARDBALL?

YEAH. THAT FAT ORANGE-STRIPED WIMP. WE KNOW HE'S IN THERE, SO WE'LL MAKE IT REAL SIMPLE. YOU THROW OUT LARDBALL. WE LEAVE, YOU DON'T, WE LEVEL THE PLACE

HMMM...

HE'S FAMILY

GARFIELD, IS THAT YOU?

THANK YOU... THAT WAS ENOUGH FUN FOR ONE DAY